Brain Games

PATTERN PUZZLES

Edward Godwin

WINDMILL BOOKS™
NEW YORK

Published in 2015 by Windmill Books, An Imprint of Rosen Publishing,
29 East 21st Street, New York, NY 10010

Text: Edward Godwin, Jane Moseley, and Jackie Strachan (JMS Books llp)
Illustrations: Memo Angeles and Others/ Shutterstock
Original design concept: Notion Design
Design: cbdesign
Editors: Joe Harris with Frances Evans

Library of Congress Cataloging-in-Publication Data

Godwin, Edward.
Pattern puzzles / by Edward Godwin.
p. cm. — (Brain games)
Includes index.
ISBN 978-1-4777-5446-7 (library binding)
1. Puzzles — Juvenile literature. 2. Mathematical recreations — Juvenile
literature. I. Godwin, Edward Xavier. II. Title.
QA95.G585 2015
793.7—d23

Printed in the United States

SL004336US

CPSIA Compliance Information: Batch #CW15WM: For further information contact Rosen
Publishing, New York, New York at 1-800-237-9932

CONTENTS

FLOWER POWER

Can you work out the next number in the pattern?

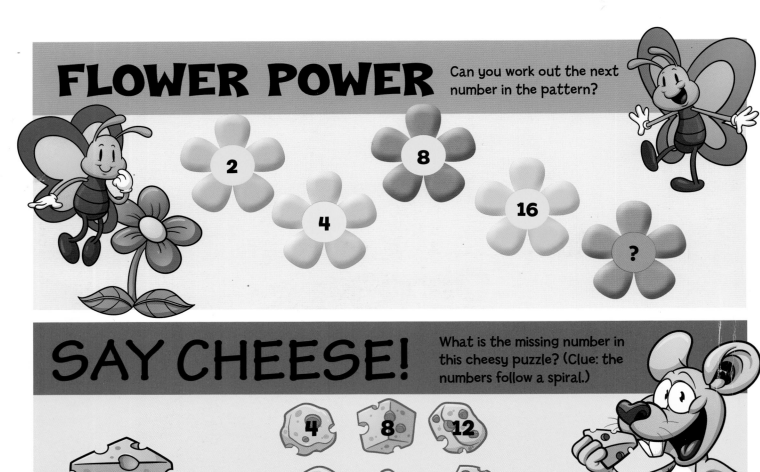

2 4 8 16 ?

SAY CHEESE!

What is the missing number in this cheesy puzzle? (Clue: the numbers follow a spiral.)

4 8 12
32 36 16
28 24 ?

TREASURE TROVE

Can you work out which number is missing from each group of coins? Remember to check your answers!

7   1   3   ?   2   ?
  14   11   17
4   ?   1   5   8   1

A   B   C

4

PYRAMID POSER

Can you work out which number goes at the top of the third pyramid?

10
3   7

9
6   3

?
8   4

PAINTER'S PROBLEM

Find the number that completes this pattern.

2   3   5   9   ?

HONEYCOMB TEASER

Which number is the odd one out?

47   15   35
   11   22

PIRATE GOLD

What do the square and the diamond have in common? The answer will give you the value of the middle coin. You can check your solution at the back!

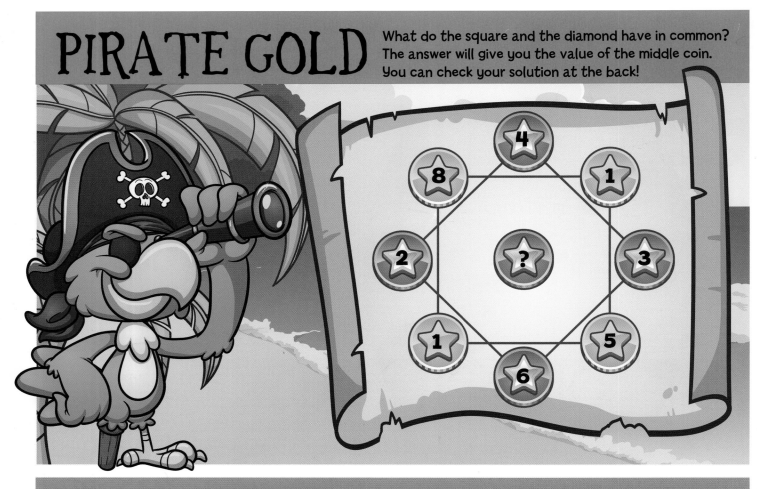

RING-A-DING-DING

Which of the rings on the left fits into the middle of the pattern? (Clue: look at both sides of the pattern.)

DOUGHNUT DELIGHT!

Which number is missing from the blue doughnut? (Clue: look at the numbers in the same positions!)

7   1
2   5

9   4
6   ?

2   3
4   4

⚽ ON THE BALL

Can you work out which number goes on the top of pile C?

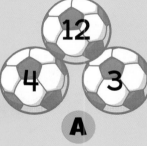

12
4   3

A

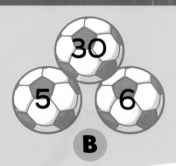

30
5   6

B

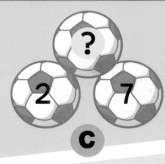

?
2   7

C

3   2   5
6   1   7
5   4   ?

RIBBIT, RIBBIT...

Take a careful look at the lily pads. Can you find the missing number?

BUSY BEES

Using the same rule for every row, can you find the missing numbers?

A	7	10	9	12	11	14
B	8	11	10	?	12	15
C	2	?	4	7	6	9
D	4	7	?	9	8	11
E	5	8	7	10	?	12
F	1	4	3	6	5	?

CANDY CORNER

Look at the numbers at the corners of both squares and at the number in middle. What's missing?

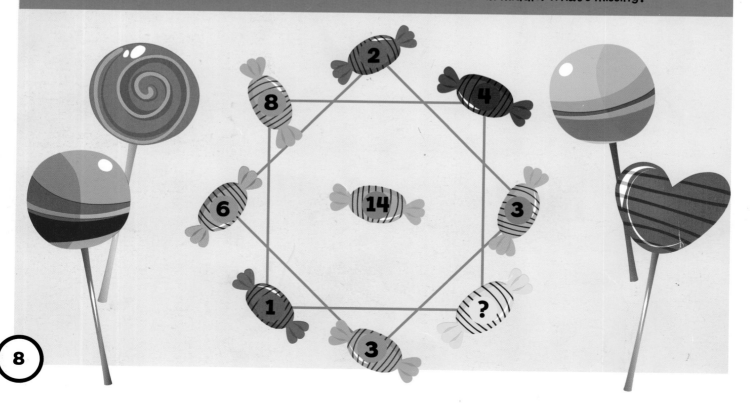

DOTTY DILEMMA

Which of the six blue dominoes completes this dotty sequence?

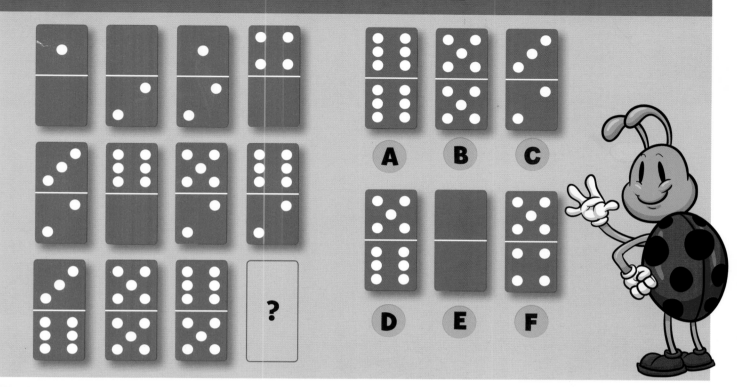

A B C

D E F

DIAMOND MINE

Can you work out which of the pink diamonds on the left should replace the missing diamond in the middle row? (Clue: look at both sides of the pattern.)

GOING BANANAS!

1 2 4 ? 16

Which number completes this
sequence of bananas?
Check your answer at the back!

WHEELIE GOOD FUN!

What is the missing number?
(Clue: look at the relationship between
the numbers in each segment.)

Which number is
missing from each
set of wrenches?

A   B   C

WRENCH IN THE WORKS

HAUNTED HOUSES

Using the first two houses as an example, work out which number is missing from the third house.

COOKIE MONSTERS

Look at the numbers at the corners of both squares and at the number in middle. What's missing?

11

BLOWING BUBBLES

Which of the numbers on the left will fit into the middle bubble?

ANYONE FOR TENNIS?

Find the missing number for the empty tennis ball. (Clue: there are two squares. Look at the corners of each one.)

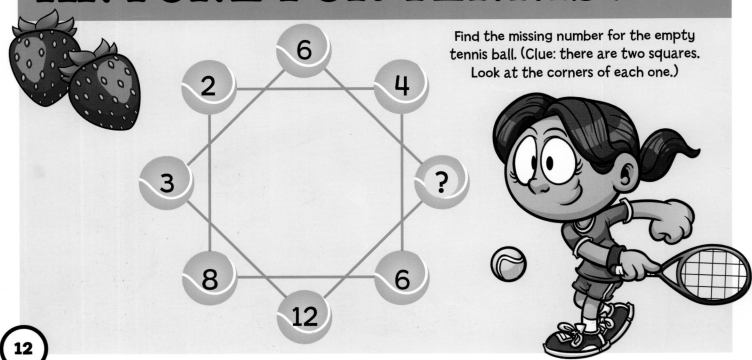

DOWN ON THE FARM

What is missing from the empty hay bale? (Clue: your subtraction skills might come in handy here!)

124	481	357
611	749	138
295	799	504
321	600	?

DIAMOND BRIGHT

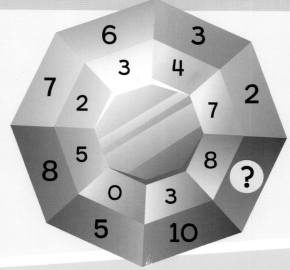

6 3
3 4
7 2 7 2
8 8
5 ?
0 3
5 10

Can you find the number that will complete the diamond pattern? Check your answer at the back when you're finished! (Clue: try adding the numbers in the diamond diagonally, for example 6 + 4.)

 49  64  75  81  100

Which egg is the odd one out?

COUNT YOUR CHICKENS

PAWPRINT POSER

3 4 7 11 18 29 ? 76

Which number must be added to complete this sequence?

STARGAZING

Can you work out which number is missing from the empty blue star?

4	3	21	1	2
6	3	81	4	5
1	1	?	9	0

Which carrot is the odd one out?

3   7   13   18   25

BAFFLED BUNNY

SPOTS BEFORE YOUR EYES!

Can you find the missing number? (Clue: look at both sides of the grid.)

4 5 6

3 2 8 9 2

1 7 5 ? 2 4 1

8 2 7 3 1

6 4 2

CASTLES IN THE SAND

8 10 9

2 ? 3

4 2 3

What is the missing number?
Remember to check your answer at the back!

15

SEEING STARS

What number should go in the yellow starfish?

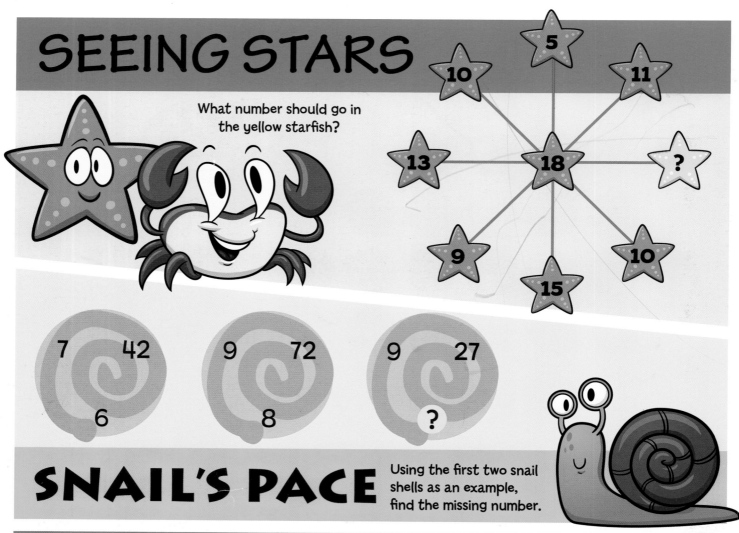

SNAIL'S PACE

Using the first two snail shells as an example, find the missing number.

GHOST STORY

Complete this scary puzzle by finding the missing number. (Clue: the puzzle works up and down as well as side to side!)

TUTTI FRUTTI...

Using the same rule for every row, can you complete this fruity pattern?

A	3	6	4	8	6	12
B	7	14	?	24	22	44
C	8	?	14	28	26	52
D	5	10	8	16	14	?
E	6	12	10	20	?	36
F	4	8	6	?	10	20

ALIEN ATTACK

Can you find the missing number?
(Clue: trace a line back and forth.)

1   2   3

13   8   5

21   34   ?

MAKING TRACKS

Which number completes this sequence of dinosaur tracks?

CRATE IT UP!

Can you work out what the missing number is? Check your solution at the back when you're finished! (Clue: the middle crate holds the key to working it out...)

BAMBOO-ZLED!

Can you find the missing number? (Clue: the puzzle works up and down as well as side to side!)

2	6	3
8	48	?
4	8	2

BOXING CLEVER

Which number completes this sequence of boxes?

4   5   7   11   ?

Which numbers are missing from two of these pair of bones?

A
7   4
5
9   12

B
11   2
?
5   8

C
?   4
11
15   12

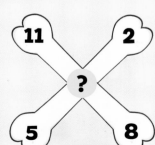

GIVE A DOG A BONE!

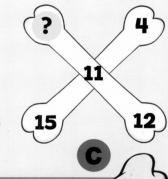

COUNTING SHEEP

Can you find the missing number? (Clue: follow a spiral, starting at the top left.)

SUNDAE SPECIALS

Which number must be added to complete this tasty sequence?

IT'S A BUG'S LIFE

Which number doesn't fit the pattern?

MAGIC STARS

Using the first two stars as a guide, can you complete this puzzle?

3
5   5
6   4

7
9   9
10   8

14
16   ?

17   15

GOLD RUSH

Can you work out which number is missing from the empty gold bar? (Clue: look at each column separately.)

1346	2159	1211
2446	3559	2911
3546	4959	4611
4646	6359	?

POOL PARTY

Which numbers are missing? (Clue: what do you do to the bottom numbers in the pink and blue rings to get the bottom number in the orange ring?)

HAVE YOUR CAKE AND EAT IT!

Which of the cakes on the right will replace the middle cake?

BUTTERFLY BALL

Look at the numbers at the corners of each square and at the number in the middle. Which number is missing from the yellow butterfly?

2
7   ?
5   20   8
3   4
5

SLAM DUNK!

5   7   8
14   3   3
1   10   ?

Complete this puzzle by finding the missing number. (Clue: try looking at the puzzle from all directions.)

Which number will complete this sticky sequence?

3   7   15   31   ?

A TASTE OF HONEY

MARTIAN MYSTERY

Which number is required to finish this puzzle?

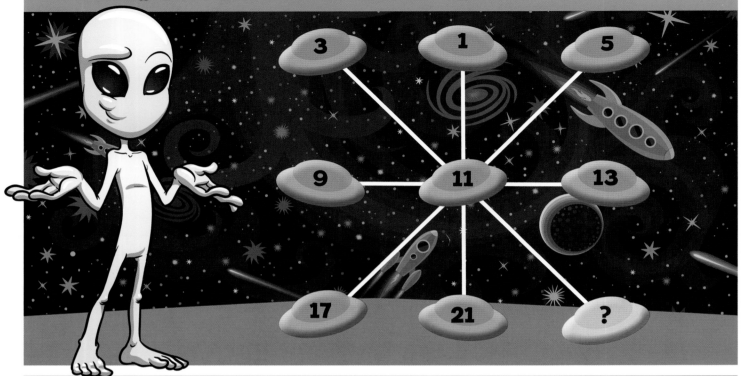

SCHOOLBOY ERROR

On each piece of paper we have added a number that doesn't belong. Which one is it?

A: 2 11 20 31 41

B: 43 13 3 19 33

C: 47 5 37 23 15

D: 53 1 17 29 39

COMPUTER VIRUS

Can you complete keypads A and B? (Clue: think of the first two columns as digits instead of numbers.)

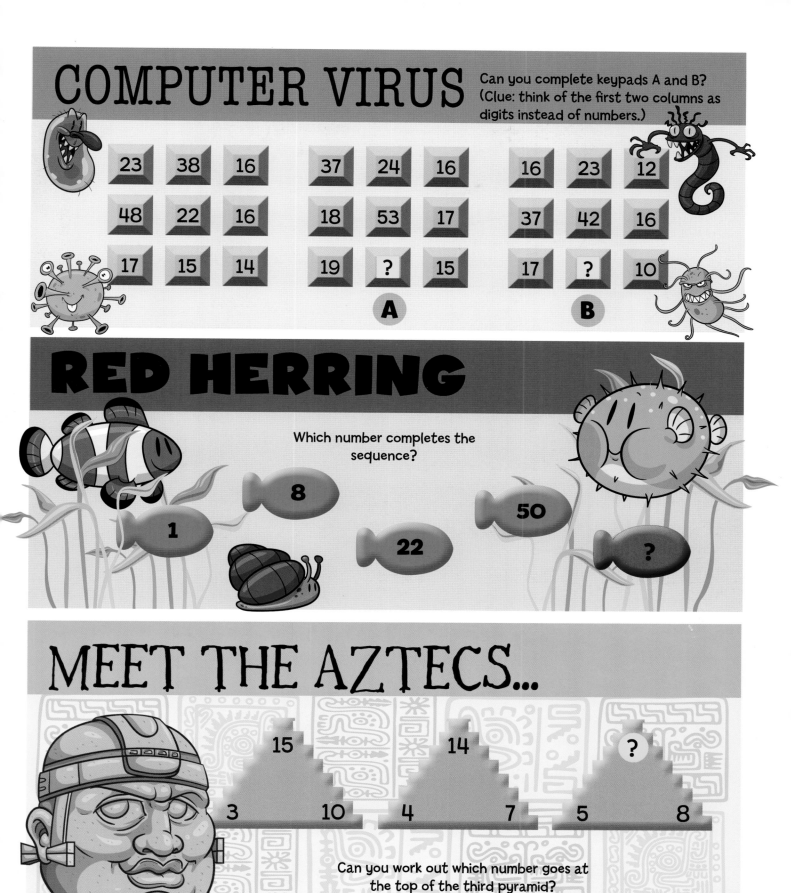

23	38	16
48	22	16
17	15	14

37	24	16
18	53	17
19	?	15

A

16	23	12
37	42	16
17	?	10

B

RED HERRING

Which number completes the sequence?

1   8   22   50   ?

MEET THE AZTECS...

15

3   10

14

4   7

?

5   8

Can you work out which number goes at the top of the third pyramid?
Check your answer at the back!

25

SOFA, SO GOOD!

Which number doesn't go with the rest?

LUCKY HORSESHOES

Complete this puzzle by finding the missing number for the middle horseshoe. (Clue: follow a spiral, starting at the top left.)

Which bluebird is the odd one out?

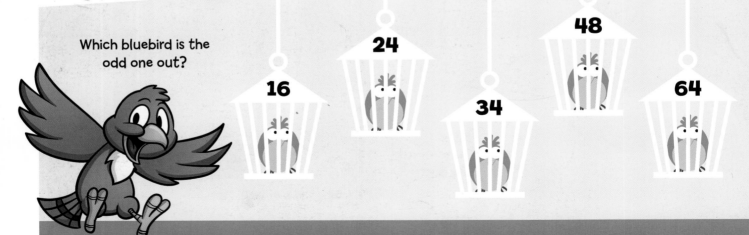

BIRDBRAIN TEASER

26

SPOOKY SPELLS

What number is missing from the middle cauldron? (Clue: it has nothing to do with adding or subtracting!)

COSMIC CAPERS

Look at the numbers at the corners of each square and at the number in the middle. Can you work out what's missing?

ANSWERS

page 4

FLOWER POWER
Answer = **32**
As you move from left to right, double the previous number to get the next one along.

SAY CHEESE!
Answer = **20**
Start with the 4 in the top left of the pattern, and move in a clockwise spiral toward the middle. The numbers follow the sequence of multiples of 4, from 4 to 36.

TREASURE TROVE
In each case, the middle number is the sum of the four outer numbers added together, so that:

A = **2** $\quad$ 4 + 7 + 1 + **2** = 14
B = **2** $\quad$ 5 + 1 + 3 + **2** = 11
C = **6** $\quad$ 1 + 8 + 2 + **6** = 17

page 5

PYRAMID POSER
Answer = **12**
Add the bottom two numbers together to get the top number.

3 + 7 = 10
6 + 3 = 9
8 + 4 = **12**

PAINTER'S PROBLEM
Answer = **17**
Double each number and subtract 1 to get the next.

HONEYCOMB TEASER
Answer = **22**
All the other numbers are odd.

page 6

PIRATE GOLD
Answer = **15**
The four numbers at the corners of the square when added together = **15**, and the four numbers which make up the diamond when added together = **15**.

RING-A-DING-DING
Answer = **6**
Add together the numbers on the left-hand side of the middle column, then add together the numbers on the right-hand side and the difference is shown in the middle.

page 7

DOUGHNUT DELIGHT!
Answer = **9**
The numbers on the blue doughnut equal the sum of the two numbers in the same position on the two purple doughnuts.

ON THE BALL
Answer = **14**
In each pile, multiply the two bottom numbers together to give the number at the top.

RIBBIT, RIBBIT...
Answer = **9**
Work across the pattern in rows. Add the numbers in the first two lily pads to get the number in the one on the right.

page 8

BUSY BEES
Line B = **13**
Line C = **5**
Line D = **6**
Line E = **9**
Line F = **8**
Moving along the rows, add 3 and then subtract 1 and continue this sequence until the end.

CANDY CORNER
Answer = **1**
There are two groups of four candies in the diagram, each defining a square. The sum of the numbers in each square is 14.

page 9

DOTTY DILEMMA
Answer = **A**
Start at the top left, and work in rows, from left to right, top to bottom. The spot total on each domino follows the sequence 1, 2, 3, 4, etc.

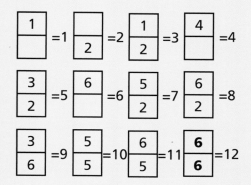

DIAMOND MINE
Answer = **3**
In each row, add up the numbers to the left of the middle column, and subtract the numbers to the right of the middle column, giving the result in the pink diamond in the middle column.

page 10

GOING BANANAS!
Answer = **8**
Multiply each number by 2 to get the next in the sequence.

WHEELIE GOOD FUN!
Answer = **3**
Multiply the two outer numbers to get the inner number in each segment.

WRENCH IN THE WORKS
Add together the two numbers at the end of each of the wrenches to get the middle number.

A = **13**
B = **9**
C = **2**

page 11

HAUNTED HOUSES
Answer = **42**
In each house, add up all the numbers in the windows and double the result, giving the number in the doorway.

COOKIE MONSTERS
Answer = **3**
The four numbers at the corners of the square when added together = 23, and the four numbers which make up the diamond when added together also = 23.

page 12

BLOWING BUBBLES
Answer = **9**
Add together the numbers on each line to find the answer in the middle column.

ANYONE FOR TENNIS?
Answer = **9**
The pattern is made from two squares. Starting with the lowest number in each square, move clockwise around the other numbers. One square contains the sequence of multiples of 2 (2, 4, 6, 8) and the other square contains multiples of 3 (3, 6, 9, 12).

page 13

DOWN ON THE FARM
Answer = **279**
In each row of the pattern, add the number on the left to the number on the right, to get the result in the middle. Or subtract the number on the left from the number in the middle.

DIAMOND BRIGHT
Answer = **7**
Start with a number from an outer segment of the diamond, and add it to the number in the inner segment, moved on one place clockwise from the outer segment. This sum is always 10.

COUNT YOUR CHICKENS
Answer = **75**
All the other numbers in the row of eggs are square numbers.

page 14

PAWPRINT POSER
Answer = **59**
Starting on the left and moving toward the right, add the previous two numbers together to get the next number.
3 + 4 = 7, 4 + 7 = 11, 7 + 11 = 18.

STARGAZING
Answer = **18**
In each row, add up separately the numbers on the left and on the right of the blue star. Multiply the two together to get the number in the blue star.

BAFFLED BUNNY
Answer = **18**
All the other numbers are odd.

page 15

SPOTS BEFORE YOUR EYES!
Answer = **10**
In each row, add up the numbers on either side of the central column and divide this total by 2 to give the value in the middle.

CASTLES IN THE SAND
Answer = **5**
Work down through the pattern in columns. Multiply the middle number by the bottom number to get the top number.

page 16

SEEING STARS
Answer = **7**
Add together the numbers on the two starfish opposite each other, and subtract 2 to get the middle number, 18.

SNAIL'S PACE
Answer = **3**
Multiply the top left and bottom numbers together to get the top right number.

GHOST STORY
Answer = **6**
Multiply together the first and second numbers in each line to get the third.
2 x 3 = **6**
3 x 1 = 3
6 x 3 = 18

page 17

TUTTI FRUTTI...
Line B = **12**
Line C = **16**
Line D = **28**
Line E = **18**
Line F = **12**
Moving along each row, multiply the first number on the left by 2, to get the second number, then subtract 2 from this to get the third number, multiply the third number by 2 to get the fourth, subtract 2 from this … and continue this sequence.

ALIEN ATTACK
Answer = **55**
Starting with the robot in the top left corner, move along the row to the right. At the end of the row, move down one row and head to the left. At the end of this row, move down to the last row and head to the right. Add together the first two numbers to get the next one. So, 1 + 2 = 3, 2 + 3 = 5, etc.

page 18

MAKING TRACKS
Answer = **10**
Moving from left to right, add 2 for the next number, then subtract 1 for the next and continue this sequence.

CRATE IT UP!
Answer = **4**
In each crate, add the three outer numbers together and divide by 3 to get the inner number.

page 19

BAMBOO-ZLED!
Answer = **6**
Multiply the first and third numbers in each row and column to get the number in the middle.

BOXING CLEVER
Answer = **19**
Multiply each number by 2 and then subtract 3 to get the next number.

GIVE A DOG A BONE!
The middle number in each case is the difference between the numbers on either end of the diagonal lines:
B = **3**
C = **1 or 23**

page 20

COUNTING SHEEP
Answer = **7**
Starting in the top left corner and moving clockwise in a spiral pattern toward the middle, add 2 for the next number, subtract 1 for the next, add 2, subtract 1, etc.

SUNDAE SPECIALS
Answer = **19**
Working from left to right, the numbers represent the sequence of prime numbers.

IT'S A BUG'S LIFE
Answer = **15**
All other numbers in the row are the cube numbers of 1, 2, 3, and 4.

MAGIC STARS
Answer = **16**
Starting with the top number and moving clockwise, add 2 to get the next number, then subtract 1, add 2, and then finally subtract 1 again.

GOLD RUSH
Answer = **6311**
Work through the pattern in columns, from top to bottom. In the left-hand column, add 1,100 to each number as you go down. For the middle column, add 1,400, and for the right-hand column, add 1,700.

page 22

POOL PARTY
Answer = **6** and **6**
The numbers in each of the segments in the bottom rings are equal to double the numbers in the matching segments in the corresponding positions of the two rings immediately above.

HAVE YOUR CAKE AND EAT IT!
Answer = **7**
In each row, add together the numbers on either side of the central column and divide it by 2 to get the middle number.

page 23

BUTTERFLY BALL
Answer = **6**
The four numbers at the corners of the square when added together equal 20, and the four numbers which make up the diamond when added together also equal 20.

SLAM DUNK!
Answer = **9**
If you add up the numbers in any row or column, their total is always 20.

A TASTE OF HONEY
Answer = **63**
Moving from left to right, double each number and add 1 to give the next number along.

page 24

MARTIAN MYSTERY
Answer = **19**
The middle number is equal to the numbers opposite each other added together and divided by two.

SCHOOLBOY ERROR
A = **20**
B = **15**
C = **33**
D = **39**
All the rest are prime numbers (numbers that are only divisible by themselves and 1).

page 25

COMPUTER VIRUS
Answer: A = **14** and B = **11**
The numbers in the third keys in each row and column are the sum of the digits in the first two keys.

RED HERRING
Answer = **106**
Add 3 to each number and double it to get the next.

MEET THE AZTECS...
Answer: **20**
Multiply the bottom two numbers and halve the result to get the top number.

page 26

SOFA, SO GOOD!
Answer = **93**
All other numbers are multiples of 9.

LUCKY HORSESHOES
Answer = **8**
Starting in the top left corner and moving clockwise in a spiral pattern towards the middle, add 3 for the next number, subtract 2, and continue this sequence.

BIRDBRAIN TEASER
Answer = **34**
All the other numbers are multiples of 8.

page 27

SPOOKY SPELLS
Answer = **8131**
Reverse the numbers shown in the cauldrons on the left and right to find the number in the middle.

COSMIC CAPERS
Answer = **1**
The cosmic pattern is made from two squares. Multiplied together, the four numbers at the corners of the complete square make 24. Multiplied together, the three numbers of the other square make 24, 24 x 1 = 24.

31

GLOSSARY

Aztecs (AZ-teks) Members of the Native American people who founded Mexico.

bamboozle (bam-BOO-zuhl) To trick of confuse someone.

cauldron (KAWL-druhn) A large pot or kettle used for boiling liquid.

cosmic (KOZ-mik) Relating to the planets, stars, and space.

dilemma (dih-LEH-muh) A situation where you have to make a difficult decision.

Martian (MAHR-shuhn) Relating to the planet Mars and possible beings who live there.

pyramid (PIH-ruh-mid) A royal tomb built by Ancient Egyptians, with a square base and four triangular sides.

sequence (SEE-kwuhns) An arrangement of things in a particular order.

trove (TROHV) A collection of valuable things.

virus (VY-rus) A harmful program for computers; a disease caused by a small living thing.

FURTHER READING

Harbin-Miles, Ruth, Don Balka, and Ted Hull. *Math Games.* Huntington Beach, CA: Shell Education, 2013.

Yoder, Eric and Natalie Yoder. *One Minute Mysteries: 65 Short Mysteries You Solve With Math!* Washington, DC: Science, Naturally!, 2010.

WEBSITES

For web resources related to the subject of this book, go to:

www. windmillbooks.com/weblinks and select this book's title.

INDEX